TABLE OF CONTENTS

ACRONYMS

9/11   September 11, 2001

COIN   Counterinsurgent

IED   Improvised Explosive Device

ISAF   International Security Assistance Force

ILLUSTRATIONS

CHAPTER 1

INTRODUCTION

> We must not rely on changing the hearts and minds of terrorists. The motivation for terrorism results from long-term social, cultural and psychological pressures, which are difficult to alter. But motivation is only part of the formula for terrorism. The other is opportunity for attack that derives from the social, technical and physical features of society that facilitate acts of terrorism. Opportunity is easier to reduce than the terrorists; motivation and opportunity reduction brings more immediate protection. In any case, easy opportunities encourage terrorists to attack.
>
> — Ronald V. Clarke and Graeme R. Newman,
> *Outsmarting the Terrorists*

The Puzzle

From 2003 to 2009, the Taliban controlled the population and terrain of Zhari

District, Afghanistan. Zhari was the birthplace of the Taliban movement and was

infamous for its sweltering heat, thick green vegetation, and networked mujahedeen era

fighting positions (Matthews 2011, 132). Despite Zhari's strategic importance, the

International Security and Assistance Force (ISAF) were unable to allocate a sufficient

number of soldiers to conduct successful operations to counter the Taliban. Those

soldiers who were sent to Zhari quickly discovered why Soviet troops in the 1980s

referred to it as the green hell or heart of darkness (Matthews 2011, 132). In 2006, the 1st

Battalion, Royal Canadian Regiment conducted Operation Medusa in Zhari and were

quickly overwhelmed by large numbers of Taliban fighters operating from improved

bunker complexes across the district (Day 2008). The Taliban's knowledge of the terrain

and integrated use of indirect and direct fires resulted in the death of 19 Canadian

Soldiers (Day 2008). Canadian officers declared that the failures of Operation Medusa

1

were the result of limited combat power and more importantly, faulty intelligence analysis (Day 2008).

In 2010, ISAF and the United States sent additional combat forces into Afghanistan as a part of the troop "surge" designed to clear the Taliban from their strongholds. The increase in combat forces was complimented by an increase in intelligence personnel capable of sifting through years of reporting. Taliban compounds, fighting positions, movement routes, bunkers, and improvised explosive device (IED) caches were identified through ISAF historical reporting or real time intelligence, surveillance, and reconnaissance capabilities (Matthews 2011, 134). Intelligence analysts identified patterns of behavior and discovered the Taliban conducted their daily operations in the same manner a person in the United States would conduct their daily work routines.

The Zhari based Taliban would wake up, conduct their prayers, move along predetermined routes to weapon caches, move along predetermined routes to fighting positions, and then retreat along predetermined routes following small scale attacks. As one intelligence officer noted "So we had a . . . patterned enemy in Zhari . . . he was so comfortable with the terrain and the fact that they owned it that they just . . . became almost lazy in their movement patterns" (Matthews 2011, 134). Over the course of 2010, ISAF conducted operations in Zhari by targeting the Taliban's patterned behavior. This targeting became so successful that the Taliban became reluctant to send more fighters to Zhari and several field commanders flatly refused to conduct operations in the district (Gall 2011).

The Taliban's patterned behavior in Zhari raises several questions for military professionals. What underlay the spatial and temporal patterns of the Taliban's attacks? Why did the Taliban conduct their operations in a patterned manner? What were the causal mechanisms that drove their patterned behavior? Was the Taliban's behavior unique to their cultural identity and the geographic location of Zhari or was their behavior consistent with the behavior of insurgents in other cultures and geographic locations? Lastly, could intelligence analysts track the causal mechanisms that drove the Taliban's behavior and develop theory to help predict the decision making cycle of individual Taliban fighters or a group of fighters?

The purpose of this paper is to answer these questions by drawing on a wealth of recent criminology scholarship that has demonstrated combatant attacks are patterned within space and time (Berrebi and Lakdawalla 2006; Braithwaite and Johnson 2011; LaFree et al. 2011; Townsley, Johnson, and Ratcliffe 2008; Townsley and Oliveira 2012). These studies propose the causation of patterned attacks are related to principles of mobility, motivation, opportunity, and the sequential relationship between opposing combatants (Berrebi and Lakdawalla 2006; Braithwaite and Johnson 2011; LaFree et al. 2011; Townsley, Johnson, and Ratcliffe 2008; Townsley and Oliveira 2012). I contrast the criminology studies with Stathis N. Kalyvas's work on the casual logics behind systematic patterns of non-combatants in civil war. Kalyvas proposes that violence occurs in systematic patterns based on the level of control an actor possesses within an environment (Kalyvas 2006, 210).

I propose that the individual causal mechanisms identified in the criminology studies provide singular pieces to a larger causal puzzle. I combine the criminology

3

theories and with Kalyvas's theory on control to predict the decision making cycle of insurgents and why attacks occur within space and time. I demonstrate this theory in a visual representation that consists of eight major components. These components of control, information, frequency of attacks, combatant costs, type of attack, organizational strategy, causal mechanisms, and organizational and individual decision making processes provide a framework that proposes why spatial and temporal attack patterns occur. The conclusion of this paper utilizes this theory to depict how it can enhance traditional United States Army intelligence products.

Contributions to the Field of Military Intelligence

In January of 2010, Lieutenant General Michael T. Flynn authored a document that lamented the current state of intelligence operations in Afghanistan (Flynn, Pottinger, and Batchelor 2010). This document focused on the intelligence community's failures to adequately provide actionable intelligence to ground level users as well as deliver timely and relevant data to the highest echelons of the US government. Flynn suggested that the old methodologies utilized by the intelligence community may no longer have relevance in the highly complex environment of the modern battlefield.

This paper attempts to address the failures identified by Flynn by incorporating a multi-disciplinary academic approach to determine the causation of spatial and temporal insurgent attack patterns. Several scholarly articles have been published on the connection between crime statistics and war related attacks; however, few if any of the lessons learned from these articles have been incorporated by the military intelligence community. Combining the scholarly work in these articles with traditional military intelligence tools bridges the gap between scholar and practioner.

In addition to bringing existing scholarship to the practioner, a predictive theory is proposed in the analysis section of this paper. This theory attempts to provide intelligence officers an academic examination of attack patterns in an operational environment and define the causal mechanisms that drive insurgent behavior. This clarity provides greater situational understanding for a geographic commander and can enable them to better allocate the limited resources and manpower at their discretion.

Definitions

The backbone of this document will be based on the actors committing violent actions, the decision making process of those actors, and the patterns those violent actions result in. The actors and the processes they conduct require identification and definitions in order to logically proceed within this study. Actors who commit violence against a legitimate government authority will be referred to as insurgents throughout this paper. Insurgents will encompass actors typically known as criminals, pirates, and terrorists. The decision to refer to all violent actors as insurgents is based on the footsteps of previous studies that focus on the violent acts and motivations rather than the labels placed on the perpetrator (Braithwaite and Johnson 2011; Townsley, Johnson, and Ratcliffe 2008). This decision is also based on research that has identified consistency in the decision-making process of violent actors across a broad spectrum (Townsley and Oliveira 2012, 9).

The combatant's decision making process to commit violent acts is identified as bounded rationality. The term bounded rationality is derived from economic theory and "expressed the idea that decision making was always bounded by the constraints of an actor's situations" (Clarke and Newman 2006, 20). Bounded rationality was adopted by criminologists in their work to describe the limitations placed on combatants when planning and carrying out their operations (Clarke and Newman 2006, 20). A lack of time, limited information, limited resources, emotions, chance, and the potential for outside intervention all limit a combatant's decision when attempting to maximize their benefits.

The result of the combatant's decision making process is known as pattern of life. Pattern of life is the consistent and routine actions that combatants conduct in their daily living and operational planning. Research has shown that combatants display "remarkable consistency" in their decisions over a period of time (Clarke and Newman 2006, 87). These decisions, derived from limitations in their own lives, results in identifiable patterns that can be quantified by observers and exploited by opposition forces.

Limitations

A limitation in the study of combatants, their decision making processes, and the patterns derived from that process can be found in urban bias. Stathis N. Kalyvas utilized this term to describe urban intellectuals writing academic research on conflicts that occurred in predominantly rural areas and by predominantly peasant-like combatants (Kalyvas 2006, 38). This bias is derived from prejudices that often assume rural violence is the result of primitive cultures and leads to researchers making inaccurate interpretations of the data they are collecting. An example of this can be found in Western studies that characterize combatants as savages, psychopathic murderers, or mindless drones that are brainwashed by religious masters (Clarke and Newman 2006, 12). These terms appear time and time again to describe combatants; despite extensive

6

research that has shown their decision making process is based in bounded rationality (Wilson 2000, 404). Chapter 2 will examine multiple case studies that depict the consistency of decision making in actors across a wide range of cultures, identities, and geographic locations. The consistency in these behaviors demonstrates that some form of rationality takes place in their decision making process.

A second potential limitation on this study is the use of heuristics and biases to rule out ambiguity. Major Blair S. Williams wrote an article in September-October 2010 edition of *Military Review*, discussing the use of heuristics to reduce uncertainty and ambiguity in the military decision making process (2010, 42-52). Two specific heuristics identified by Williams that potentially impact this study are retrievability bias and search set bias.

Williams defined retrievability bias as using the frequency of past events to reinforce preconceived notions of future events (2010, 42). This paper's foundation is built off the author's recollection of events from 2010 to 2011 in Afghanistan. The behavior of the Taliban during this period appeared to be exceptionally patterned; with each subsequent significant act they conducted reinforcing the author's opinion of a patterned enemy. In order to avoid the potential of retrievability bias, this paper focuses on a wide range of studies focused on statistical data to display attack patterns. Anecdotal stories are used to reinforce statistics in the conclusion, but the remainder of the paper attempts to remain on the firm ground of statistics.

Williams defines search set bias as the heuristic that leads to a researcher only utilizing material that leads to their foredrawn conclusion (2010, 42). My research focuses on those topics and studies that provide supporting information to my original hypothesis. This initial research leads to corroborating studies and continues in a pattern that supports my initial findings. This heuristic provides a difficult challenge to researchers and this study. In order to avoid search set bias, this study sought a wide range of case studies focused on varied groups and cultures. Additionally, this study compares, contrasts, and combines a multidisciplinary approach to answer the question of what underlies spatial and temporal attack patterns.

A final limitation on this study is the availability of unclassified quantifiable attack reporting. This study focused on unclassified studies and reports that could have the potential of error in reporting on attack locations and times. This limitation is the result of a decision to avoid the use of classified material, an inability to declassify statistical attack data, and the desire to retain the unclassified nature of this study.

<u>Scope</u>

The focus of this study is on underlying causes of spatial and temporal patterns in insurgent attacks. This analysis is conducted in an effort to determine if a multi-disciplinary theory can clarify attack pattern causality. The theory is designed to serve as a tool to support the analysis of intelligence professionals, exploit the vulnerabilities of insurgent decision making, and influence the decision making process of tactical geographic commanders during combat operations.

The tactical focus of this paper excludes recent studies that have produced significant advances in the theory of violence. These studies have focused on the strategic roots of violence by focusing on ideology, culture, and cleavages (Kalyvas 2003, 475-494). Strategic solutions in the form of hearts and minds campaigns, national policy changes, and education have been recommended as potential deterrents to violence, but their implementation requires considerable time and their effectiveness remains unclear (Clarke and Newman, 2006). These solutions and their implications are important areas of study and require considerable effort that will not be covered within this paper.

The tactical nature of this study is aimed at transitioning solutions from scholarship to practitioners in the field. It does not focus on the deep motivations of why attacks occur, but on the more practical motivations of what underlies the spatial and temporal nature of attack patterns. It accomplishes this by showing that attacks are patterned within space and time and by presenting a theory that attempts that, shows opportunity is more often than not, the reason behind spatial and temporal attack patterns.

Way Ahead

This paper is divided into five chapters. Chapter 1 provides the introduction and theoretical framework for the remaining chapters. Chapter 2 utilizes research from the field of criminology to identify insurgents, their bounded rationality, and the decisions they make. This chapter is introduced with a research framework designed by Ronald V. Clarke and then followed by case studies from the Horn of Africa, Spain, and Iraq that display patterned attacks within space and time. The findings of these studies show that the planning calculus of combatants remains similar despite their differences in space and time (Townsley and Oliveira 2012, 9). Chapter 2 concludes by contrasting the theory on patterned systematic violence against non-combatants in civil wars (Kalyvas 2006, 210-245). This theory proposes the level of control an actor possesses in a geographical region results in the level of violence they will conduct against non-combatants. Chapter 3 builds on the analysis of chapter 2 and proposes a methodology that combines criminology research and Kalyvas's zones of conflict to form a theory of causation for spatial and temporal attack patterns. This theory is visually represented in chapter 4 and then unpacked in a step-by-step manner that defines its eight major components and their relationship in Kalyvas's five zones of control. The implications and applicability of the theory presented in chapter 4 are discussed in the findings section of chapter 5. Chapter 5 concludes with a recommendation for further testing of the theory developed in chapter 4.

CHAPTER 2

LITERATURE REVIEW

Why did the Taliban in Zhari, Afghanistan conduct attacks that were patterned within space and time? Why did they move along the same routes, store their weapons in the same caches, and conduct their attacks in the same locations? What factor or factors led the Taliban to make these decisions? This chapter will explore the Taliban's decisions and offer two theories on the causal logic behind them. The first theory, based on criminology, will focus on the individual actor's decision making process. The second theory, proposed by Stathis N. Kalyvas, will examine systematic patterned violence as the result of territorial control. This chapter will conclude with an analysis on the limitation of these theories and propose combining them into a new theory that has the potential to offer greater understanding of why patterned attacks occur within space and time.

Criminology Overview

The lone Taliban combatant faces a myriad of questions each day. Where should I attack? Who should I attack? When should I attack? How should I attack? Why should I attack? These questions are filtered through the insurgents' decision making process and result in action. If we are to believe the western media, this decision making process is that of a madman, a religious zealot, or a mindless drone. The logic flows that anyone willing to conduct a suicide or IED attack must be irrational. Unfortunately, these depictions cloud the minds of researchers and muddy the waters of analysis.

If the decision making process of the lone Taliban combatant is not irrational, then what is it? Criminologists have attempted to answer this puzzle by adopting their work on the decision making process of criminals (Berrebi and Lakdawalla 2006; Braithwaite and Johnson 2011; Clarke and Newman 2006; LaFree et al. 2011; Townsley, Johnson, and Ratcliffe 2008; Townsley and Oliveira 2012). This decision making process, identified as bounded rationality, claims a combatant's decision making is bounded by the limitations of their situation (Clarke and Newman 2006, 20). A lack of time, limited resources, chance, and the potential for outside intervention, limit a combatant's ability to maximize their benefits.

We can imagine the lone combatant receiving a task to conduct an attack and the limitations their situation places upon them. Did the combatant's leaders provide them with all of the information they needed? Is the combatant familiar with the area they will attack? Are they familiar with the tactics of the enemy in the area? Do they know how to use the weapons at their disposal? Does the attack require any special training or additional support? Are their external factors, potentially as mundane as the monotony of daily family life, which could interfere with the mission?

The combatant is forced to make life or death decisions based on the constraints they face, but what leads them to act? Why should a combatant, many of whom are careful with their lives, decide to conduct a violent attack? Criminologists have proposed the decision to act results from a complex relationship between motivation and opportunity (Clarke and Newman 2006, 7). Simply stated, the combatant is motivated to attack based on actual and perceived opportunities (Clarke and Newman 2006, 9). A combatant will think more about conducting IED attacks if he lives by a road highly travelled by ISAF vehicles. The same combatant's perceived opportunity to conduct road side IED attacks would significantly decrease if they lived in a remote mountain village only accessible by small trails.

Researchers indicate that opportunity, not a higher calling, is often the leading motivator in determining if an attack will occur (Clarke and Newman 2006, 5). Peer pressure, a sense of belonging, excitement, status, economic, political, cultural, and ideological motivators all have the potential to drive behavior, but no more than the perceived opportunity to conduct an attack (Clarke and Newman 2006, 5). This immediate motivation to accomplish the task at hand is identified as a reason why attack patterns across a wide range of cultural and geographic cases appear to be consistent with one another (Clarke and Newman 2006, 6).

We determined that our combatant makes decisions based on constraints and decides to act based on the perception of opportunity, but how do they select the target location of their attacks? We know that the combatant wants to complete the task as quickly as possible and we know they can only attack where they perceive an opportunity. These criteria result in the proximity of the target being the most important characteristic to combatants (Clarke and Newman 2006, 139). A target located within close proximity to a combatant's home makes an attack routine, provides shorter distances to travel, and minimizes their exposure to capture.

Using this theory, the criminologist Michael Townsley conducted a case study to determine if attacks in Iraq clustered in space and time (Townsley, Johnson, and Ratcliffe 2008, 139). Townsley argued that attacks would cluster because it was an efficient way to operate. This efficiency, based on the least effort principle (Zipf 1949), suggested combatants would conduct attacks within close proximity to one another to decrease their exposure to capture while also maintaining familiarity with the target location.

Townsley collected three months of data from attacks in Iraq covering 4 February 2004 to 30 April 2004. This time frame provided over 2,000 attack records of which 916 were labeled as IED (Townsley, Johnson, and Ratcliffe 2008, 142). Focusing on IED attacks, Townsley "applied an epidemiological model of infectious diseases to test for communicability of future risk" (Townsley, Johnson, and Ratcliffe 2008, 142).

The results of Townsley's research are displayed in figure 1. This figure shows three tables of IED attacks that use the same criteria for time, but vary on distance. The color shaded areas represent those periods of times where attack frequencies were elevated. The darker shaded areas display the most likely occurrence of follow on attacks and indicate that an IED attack was most likely to be followed by a second attack within two days and within one kilometer from the original attack location.

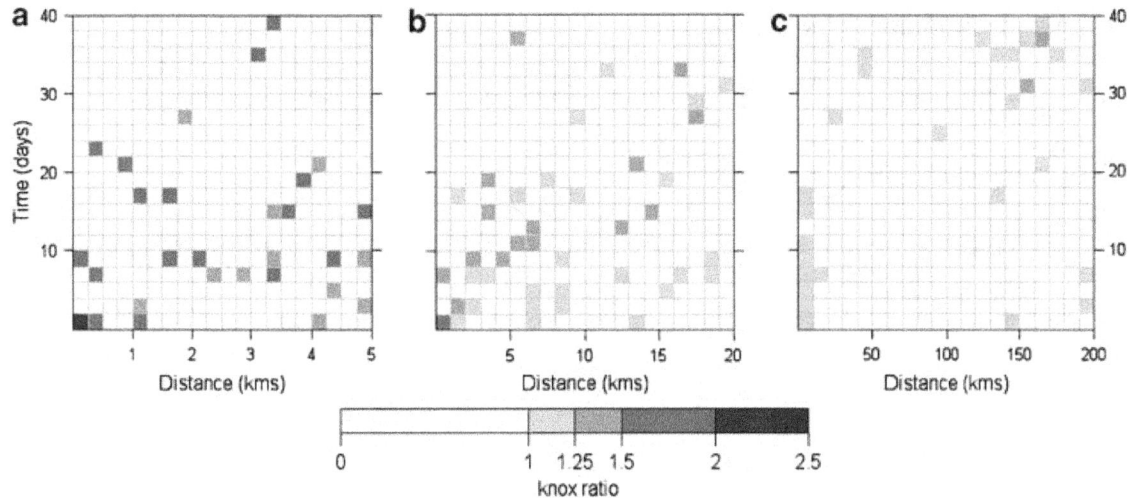

Figure 1. Townsley Attack Data

Source: Michael Townsley and Alessandro Oliveira, "Space Time Dynamics of Insurgent Activity in Iraq," *Security Journal* (2008): 21.

The patterns identified in Townsley's research appeared to be consistent with his claim that attacks would cluster in space and time. His study attributed these patterns to the combatant's use of the least effort principle and their desire to conduct efficient operations (Townsley, Johnson, and Ratcliffe 2008, 144). Townsley did offer the potential for other causal reasons for the attack patterns, but stated that the simplest explanation for the observed patterns was that the insurgents were constrained by space and time and therefore selected their targets in a rational fashion (Townsley, Johnson, and Ratcliffe 2008, 144).

Townsley followed his research on Iraq with an analysis of the space time dynamics of maritime piracy. In this research, Townsley proposed an enhanced view of the least effort principle known as the optimal foraging principle. Borrowed from wildlife ecology, the optimal foraging principle states that animals will seek nourishment in a manner that minimizes the distance they travel, the time it takes to hunt, and the effort exerted in the hunting process in order to limit their own risk of death or injury (Townsley and Oliveira 2012, 3).

We can imagine our Taliban combatant using the optimal foraging principle in their effort to locate a target that offers them the lowest amount of risk while at the same time meeting their minimal objectives. Townsley used this same principle in his exploration of piracy and proposed the optimum foraging principle in combination with bounded rationality would result in pirates conducting their attacks in clusters within space and time (Townsley and Oliveira 2012, 3).

Townsley collected six years of pirate activity from attacks in the horn of African covering 2006 until 2011. This time frame provided over 500 attacks identified in space and time. Townsley applied the same technique utilized in his previous study on Iraq to determine the communicability of pirate attacks (Townsley and Oliveira 2012, 5-9).

The results of Townsley's research demonstrated that pirate attacks occurred in clusters within space and time. These clusters appeared consistent with the attack patterns of insurgents in Iraq and indicated that the behaviors of both groups employed a similar decision making process (Townsley and Oliveira 2012, 9). Each group attempted to satisfy their needs, but did so in a manner that minimized their own risk.

Townsley's case studies on insurgent and pirate attacks provide insight on the decision making process of combatants, but they fail to address the behavior of the combatant's rival. It is one thing for our combatant to live next to a road, but that road requires a rival force to utilize it in order for a true attack opportunity to occur. The actor using the least effort principle and the optimum forager principle cannot conduct attacks if a rival does not operate in their vicinity.

In 2011, Alex Braithwaite and Shane D. Johnson explored the potential correlation of counterinsurgent (COIN) operations and insurgent attacks in Iraq (2011, 32). Following in the footsteps of Townsley, the authors accepted that IED attacks occurred in clusters in space and time, but argued that the least effort principle and optimal foraging were not the only causes of patterned attacks. The authors proposed COIN operations cluster in space and time, that COIN operations cluster following IED attacks, and that COIN operations have the effect of provoking IEDs at proximate locations and times (Braithwaite and Johnson 2011, 31).

Braithwaite and Johnson's hypotheses provide a clear logic for the combatant to follow. The combatant will conduct attacks where COIN operations occur (preferably located in close proximity to the combatant), will monitor the patterned response of COIN operations following an attack, and will attempt to exploit those patterns by conducting repeat attacks in the same location. The optimum forager and least effort principles are retained, but rely on the behavior of their rival forces.

Braithwaite and Johnson tested their theory by drawing from a data set of attacks from January to June 2005. This time period provided a data set of over 3,700 reported IED attacks (Braithwaite and Johnson 2011, 36-37). The attack data was compared against four additional data sets that displayed the most common COIN operations from the same time period (Braithwaite and Johnson 2011, 36-37). These common operations were identified as IED found, cordon and search, cache found, and raids (Braithwaite and Johnson 2011, 36-37).

Figure 2 shows the results of the spatial distribution of the author's data sets on a map designed with 5 km x 5 km cells (Braithwaite and Johnson 2011, 39). The maps coloration shows the number of events that occurred in a location with the darker colors indicating a higher frequency of events (Braithwaite and Johnson 2011, 39). The maps offer a startling visual representation that demonstrates COIN and insurgent attacks cluster in space and time. The locational data of these attacks also appear to correlate with geography, population, and Iraq's infrastructure. This further supports previous studies that indicate the non-random distribution of attacks across space (Braithwaite and Johnson 2011, 46).

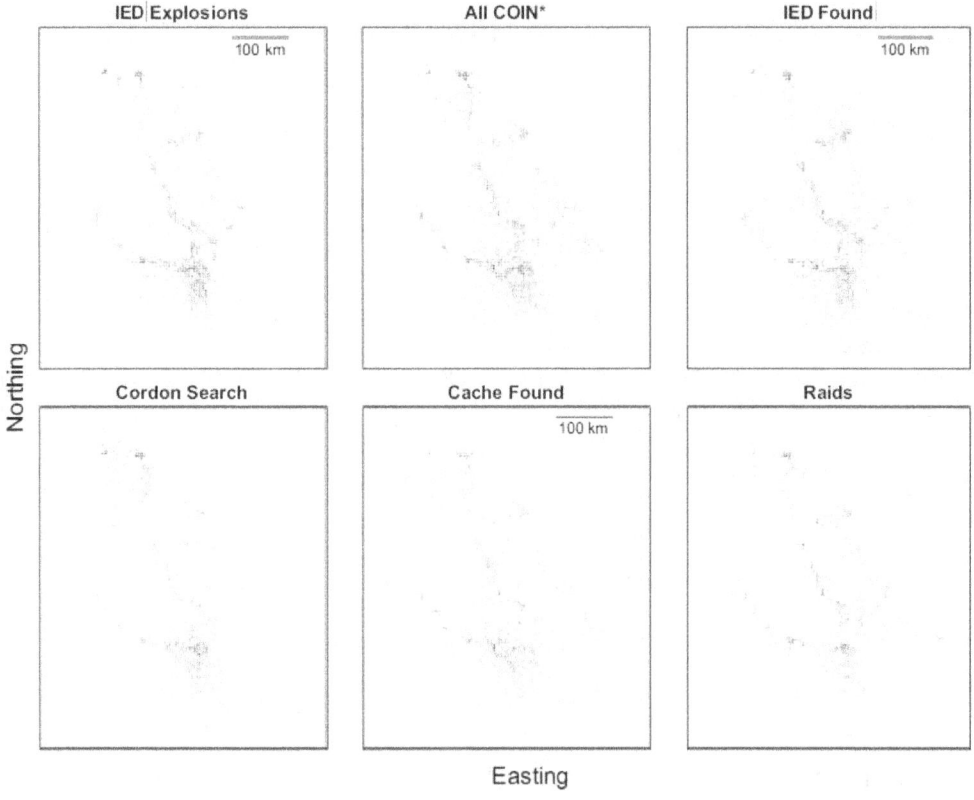

Figure 2.   Braithwaite Patterned Activity

Source: Alex Braithwaite and Shane D. Johnson, "Space-Time Modeling of Insurgency and Counterinsurgency in Iraq" *J Quant Criminol*, no. 28 (November 2011): 39.

Braithwaite and Johnson employed a second analysis of the relationship between COIN operations and insurgent attacks by using the same model as Townsley in his study on insurgent attacks in Iraq and piracy in the Horn of Africa. Figure 3 displays the Univiriate Knox analyses of six event types and the likelihood they would be followed by an IED attack. The colored areas represent IED attack occurrences and the darker shaded areas represent greater frequencies of attacks.

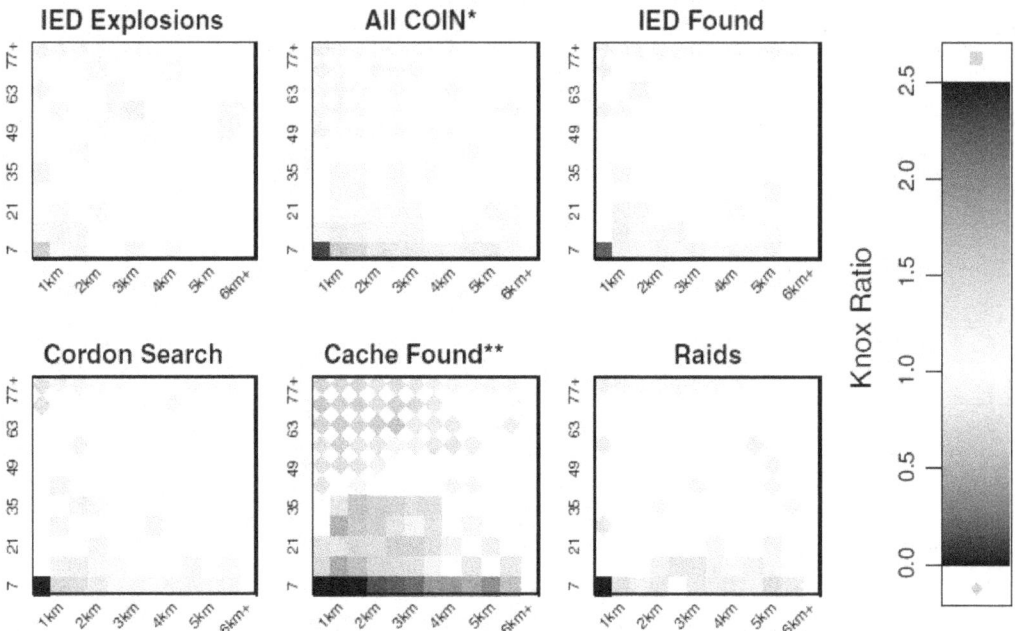

Figure 3.   Braithwaite Attack Data

Source: Alex Braithwaite and Shane D. Johnson, "Space-Time Modeling of Insurgency and Counterinsurgency in Iraq," *J Quant Criminol*, no. 28 (November 2011): 42.

The results in the table demonstrate that Braithwaite and Johnson's hypotheses appear to be true. COIN operations cluster in space and time, COIN operations cluster following IED attacks, and COIN operations provoke IEDs at proximate locations and times. Across the chart, IED events are most likely to occur within seven days and within one kilometer of a previous operation or attack occurring (Braithwaite and Johnson 2011, 43). This data provides remarkable evidence that insurgency events cluster in space and in time and that they are extremely likely to follow COIN operations.

The theories presented thus far provide a compelling example of the decision making process and a combatant's target selection. The combatant's decision making process is bounded by their situation, their decision to act is based on their perceived notions of motivation and opportunity, their attacks are driven by a desire to be efficient, and their attack location is determined by the area their rivals most often inhabit. These theories provide a clean decision making process for the single combatant, but do not take into account that the who, what, where, when, and why to attack are often decided by a combatant group.

The decision making process of a lone actor is a very different process from the decision making of a group. We can imagine our combatant is now in a room with multiple other combatants. Each individual brings their own constraints to the group and impacts it in terms of risks, rewards, and the valuation of outcomes (Clarke and Newman 2006, 70). The combatant group must reach a decision about how to maximize their efforts and it must be done in unison in order to avoid confusion (Clarke and Newman 2006, 71). The very nature of the group impacts this decision by potentially insulating members from the strategy of their superiors or enhancing it by providing information that a lone combatant could not know.

The decision making process of a combatant organization, such as the *Euskadi ta Askatasuna* (ETA), can provide additional insight on why attacks cluster in space and time. It may also help explain why certain attacks appear to be inefficient for the individual combatant, but may in actuality be very efficient for the group as a whole. In 1978 the ETA announced that they would shift their attack strategy from one that sought to keep the Spanish government out of the Basque homeland to one that sought to attrit the will of the Spanish government outside of the Basque homeland (LaFree et al. 2011, 7). Prior to 1978, the attacks conducted by the ETA were focused within the Basque territories and occurred in clusters in space and time. After 1978, the Basque began conducting less frequent, but more spectacular attacks outside of the Basque territory (LaFree et al. 2011, 7). These attacks were diffused in their location and occurred at less frequent times.

Gary LaFree conducted a study of ETA attacks from 1970 to 2007 and discovered that the ETA's strategic goals prior to 1978 and after 1978 dictated the frequency of attack patterns in space and time (LaFree et al. 2011, 25). LaFree characterized the attacks prior to 1978 as control attacks designed to maintain ETA's control of the Basque homeland (LaFree et al. 2011, 25). These attacks followed in the principles of least effort and foraging by offering the ETA attack opportunities in locations near to their base of operations. They were designed to target the Spanish government in locations where they frequented and where they attempted to penetrate into the Basque homeland (LaFree et al. 2011, 11). The attacks following the 1978 strategic shift were characterized as attrition attacks with the goal of wearing down the will of the Spanish government. These attacks occurred at symbolic locations far away from the ETA's base of operations (LaFree et al. 2011, 12). This resulted in the organization taking additional time to organize, plan, travel, and conduct their attacks in an effort to avoid capture. In turn, attacks became less frequent and varied greatly in their location.

Lafree's study on the ETA provides insight into why individual combatants may conduct attacks outside the normal foraging or least effort principle range (Lafree et al. 2011, 25). This study shows that the group's strategic decision making may supersede that of the individual actor and may result in attacks that fall outside of predicted patterns.

The field of criminology provides a theory for individual combatant decision making, on the determination of the combatant to act, on the location where the combatant desires to attack, on the relationship between attack locations and rival actors, and on the potential influences of organizational decision making on attack patterns. These theories provide one side of examining why violence occurs in patterns. The next section will look at Stathis N. Kalyvas and his theory on systematic patterns of violence.

Kalyvas Overview

Kalyvas's influential work *The Logic of Violence in Civil War* (2006) proposes that the interaction between actors operating at different levels results in the production of violence against non-combatants in a systematic and predictable way. This interaction, as Kalyvas identifies it, is the level of control rival actors possess in a given area. He defines control as the presence of, or the access enjoyed by, political actors in a given space and time. An actor possesses control of a region if they can significantly reduce the likelihood that events will occur in certain areas at certain times (Kalyvas 2006, 210).

The level of control an actor possesses in an area directly results in the level of information the actor possesses. In areas of high control, the actor possesses a high degree of information. In areas of low control, the actor possesses a low degree of information. The level of information results in an actor's ability to conduct discriminative violence in areas of high control and indiscriminative violence in areas of low control (Kalyvas 2006, 210-245).

Kalyvas designed a five-zone measure to capture the levels of control possessed in a particular area. In Zone 1 the incumbents exercise total control. They have destroyed insurgent cells, driven off armed combatants, and have the capability to prevent insurgents from operating within the zone's borders. The incumbent possesses a high degree of information within the zone and are capable of influencing potential insurgents with the mere threat of violence (Kalyvas 2006, 218).

Zone 5 is the inverse of Zone 1 and is in the total control of the insurgent. These base areas are locations where insurgent forces operate openly with minimal or no government influence (Kalyvas 2006, 218). The insurgent assumes the role of shadow government in Zone 5 and provides policing and essential services to the population. Sadr City in Eastern Baghdad provides a recent example of a location that fits this description. The Sadrists provided policing, charity, medical, and food support to their population and exercised total control within their borders.

Zone 2 is predominantly controlled by the incumbent, but their control is incomplete (Kalyvas 2006, 224). Insurgents enjoy limited access to Zone 2, but are not free to operate openly. The incumbent possesses a high degree of information in this zone and retains the ability to target discriminately. Zone 4 is the mirror opposite of Zone 2 with the insurgent exercising secure, but incomplete control (Kalyvas 2006, 224). Zone 4 offers the insurgent a high degree of control and the ability to discriminately target incumbent operatives.

Zone 3 is a geographical area where both actors enjoy equal levels of control. Zone 3 locations are known as the contested areas in war and are often the location of the front lines (Kalyvas 2006, 212). Violence against civilians in this area is often indiscriminate due to a lack possessed by the incumbent and insurgent. The population is caught in the crossfire and typically attempts to remain passively neutral and desire to be level alone (Kalyvas 2006, 223-227).

Kalyvas's predicted that violence in these zones would occur according to the level of control possessed by an actor. The higher the level of an actor's control, the less likely the actor would result to violence. This led Kalyvas to predict there would be limited or no violence by incumbents in zone 1 or insurgents in Zone 5. Kalyvas further predicted that the lower level of an actor's control, the more likely it would result in indiscriminate violence. Thus, insurgent violence in Zones 1 and 2 and incumbent violence in Zones 4 and 5 would be indiscriminate. Under incomplete control, Kalyvas predicted that violence would be selective in Zone 2 by the incumbent and Zone 4 by the insurgent. Finally, in Zone 3, Kalyvas predicted that a lack of information would result in indiscriminate violence by both the incumbent and the insurgent (Kalyvas 2006, 204).

Kalyvas tested his predictions against a data set he collected in the Argolid region of southern Greece from the Greek Civil War (Kalyvas 2006, 247-248). The Argolid consists of sixty-one villages that are spread across diverse terrain and economic status. The region is rural, dominated by farms, and most land is owned by those who work on it (Kalyvas 2006, 253). The great majority of inhabitants of the Argolid are Christian Orthodox with half of the population comprised of those from Albanian descent (Kalyvas 2006, 254).

The results from Kalyvas's test on the Argolid confirmed his predictions and showed that dominant but incomplete zones of control were most likely to see selective violence by the controlling group. The results also showed the volume of violence was higher in Zones 2 and 4 when compared with zones of total control (Kalyvas 2006, 328). Surprisingly, Zone 3 possessed a lower degree of civilian violence that Kalyvas attributed to the villages denouncing violence for fear of the population using the insurgent and incumbent as a method to conduct reprisals and counter reprisals.

Kalyvas's work in The Logic of Violence in Civil War offers a distinct theory on why and where patterned violence occurs. Levels of incumbent and insurgent control, their relationship to information, and the use of information to conduct discriminate or indiscriminate violence against civilians provide a potential correlation to the study of combatant on combatant violence highlighted in the previous criminology section.

Conclusion

A wealth of criminology literature shows that attacks occur in patterns within space and time. This literature focuses on the decision making process of combatants and of combatant groups. The least effort principle, the optimum foraging principle, the sequential relationship between rivals, and the strategic goals of an organization all impact the actions of combatants and lead to patterned behavior. The authors of these individual works have each accepted that their singular theories are perhaps one of many reasons why patterned violence occurs. In essence, each theory presents singular piece to the puzzle of why patterned violence occurs, but when examined together they present a more complete picture.

Kalyvas presents an alternate view on systematic violence and focuses on non-combatant attacks in zones of control. Kalyvas demonstrates the validity of his theory with a case study on Greece and shows that violence against non-combatants has a clear relationship with an actor's level of control within a geographic area. This study, while valuable, does not provide evidence on combatant vs combatant violence in zones of control. Kalyvas's study is also focused within the world of political science and does not take into account the work conducted on systematic violence by criminologists.

This remainder of this paper will propose a theory that combines the causal logics discovered in criminology with Kalyvas's theory on zones of control. I propose a theory that displays two sets of causal mechanisms focusing on the ground-level decision making of combatants and the organizational and strategic interests of the insurgent group. This theory explains how these two different drivers result in greater overall picture of why attacks that clusters in space and time.

CHAPTER 3

RESEARCH METHODOLOGY

The purpose of this study is to determine what causal mechanisms underlie the spatial and temporal patterns of insurgent attacks. The paper is an exercise in theory development and accomplishes this by examining attack patterns and causal factors. It combines them in a multi-disciplinary theory that depicts the decision making process of why insurgents conduct attacks in spatial and temporal patterns.

This chapter will explain the methodology utilized to create the theory in chapter 4. It will identify the criteria used to select the criminology case studies and the causal mechanisms found within the theory. It will provide insight on the inclusion of Kalyvas's theory on systematic patterned violence. The chapter will conclude with a summary on how the criminology and Kalyvas's theories are combined to create a new theory on patterned violence.

The criminology case studies identified in chapter 2 provide a compelling argument that attacks cluster in space and time. These case studies utilize data from the Horn of Africa, Iraq, and Spain to show that actors across a wide geographical and cultural divide offend in similar manners. Each of these case studies also offers individual causal mechanisms as the driver for the offender's behavior. Chapter 2 discussed the limitation of these individual theories and predicts that their combination could provide additional value to intelligence professionals. Chapter 4 combines these causal mechanisms with an additional study from Israel to present a theory of causation across zones of control. The case studies in Israel, Spain, and the Horn of Africa were also selected because they are outside of the author's operational expertise and present a counter to any selection set bias.

The criminology case studies repeatedly identified the importance of geography concerning the proximity in the selection of target locations. These repeated references led the author to re-examine Kalyvas's work on the systematic and patterned violence against non-combatants in civil wars. Kalyvas proposed that control in geographic areas had a direct result on attacks against non-combatants (Kalyvas 2006). Kalyvas's inclusion in this study provided a clean framework to apply the causal mechanisms of criminology across a series of defined geographic areas.

The proposed theory in chapter 4 is to the author's knowledge; the first time civil war literature from political science and repeat offender literature from criminology have been combined to form a new theory on what underlies the spatial and temporal patterns of insurgent attacks. The proposed theory utilizes eight major components that were prevalent in both sets of literature to create a visual representation that depicts the individual and organizational decision making process of when and where insurgents conduct attacks. This visual representation of the theory uses Kalyvas's zones and displays how causal factors are influenced in each zone.

The theory in chapter 4 is also designed to support intelligence officers and influence the decision making process of tactical commanders. The theory offers potential causal reasoning for why attacks occur when and where they do. The theory also identifies potential points of friction in the insurgent's decision making process. These points of friction offer potential sources of exploitation in countering an insurgent organization's attacks.

Chapter 4 will begin by unpacking each component of the theory and then providing an example of how each component influences Kalyvas's zones of control. Real world locations were selected that display the qualities of Zones 5, 3, and 1 and each location offers significant support for the chapter's proposed theory.

CHAPTER 4

ANALYSIS

The literature presented in this study demonstrates that attacks cluster within space and time. The field of criminology proposes a series of causal mechanisms that underlie the spatial and temporal patterns of these attacks. These causal mechanisms include the least effort principle, the optimum foraging principle, the sequential relationship between rivals, and the strategic goals of an organization. These theories are presented in individual studies and acknowledge their limitations as singular causal mechanisms of patterned violence. Kalyvas provides an alternate view on attacks and proposes that the interaction between actors operating at different levels results in the production of violence against non-combatants in a systematic and predictable way (Kalyvas 2006, 210). Kalyvas's theory and the theories found in criminology offer an exceptional level of insight on the causes of patterned violence, but unfortunately they have had little exposure in the military profession.

The purpose of this study is to identify the underlying cause of spatial and temporal violence in insurgent attacks. In order to do this, I propose combining the theories of criminology and applying them to Kalyvas's five zone model. This new theory retains Kalyvas's theories based on control and information, but transitions the focus of violence to combatant against combatant attacks. Using the causal mechanisms identified in criminology literature, the theory shows where the individual combatant wants to conduct their attacks, the strategy they employ behind those attacks, the costs associated with those attacks, the frequency in which the attacks will occur, and the potential conflict that may arise between the individual combatant's decision making process and the combatant's organizational decision making process.

This chapter will start by presenting a visual representation of a theory on the individual and organizational decision making of insurgents and then transition to defining the theory behind the visual representation. The theory will be explained by breaking down the eight major components of the visual representation and then providing an explanation of how those components integrate with Kalyvas's five zones of control. The chapter will conclude by proposing an answer to this paper's research question.

The theory displayed in figure 4 is a visual representation of the decision making process of insurgents and insurgent groups. The theory is designed from the insurgent's point of view and consists of eight major components. These components are the level of control, level of information, frequency of attacks, combatant costs, type of attack, organizational strategy, causal mechanisms, and organizational and individual decision making processes. The components are overlaid on Kalyvas's five zones and change accordingly to each zone. These changes will be explained in detail later in this chapter within component and zone by zone explanation.

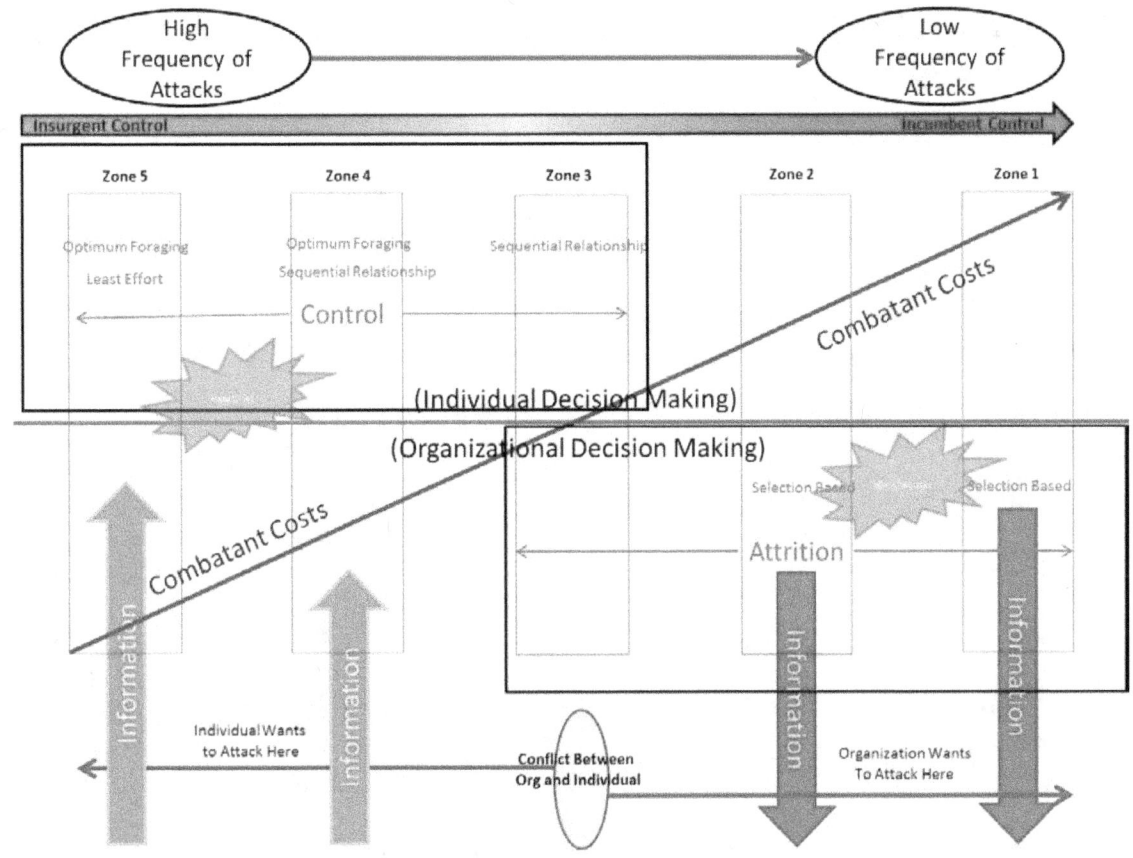

Figure 4.   Insurgent Decision Making

Source: Created by author.

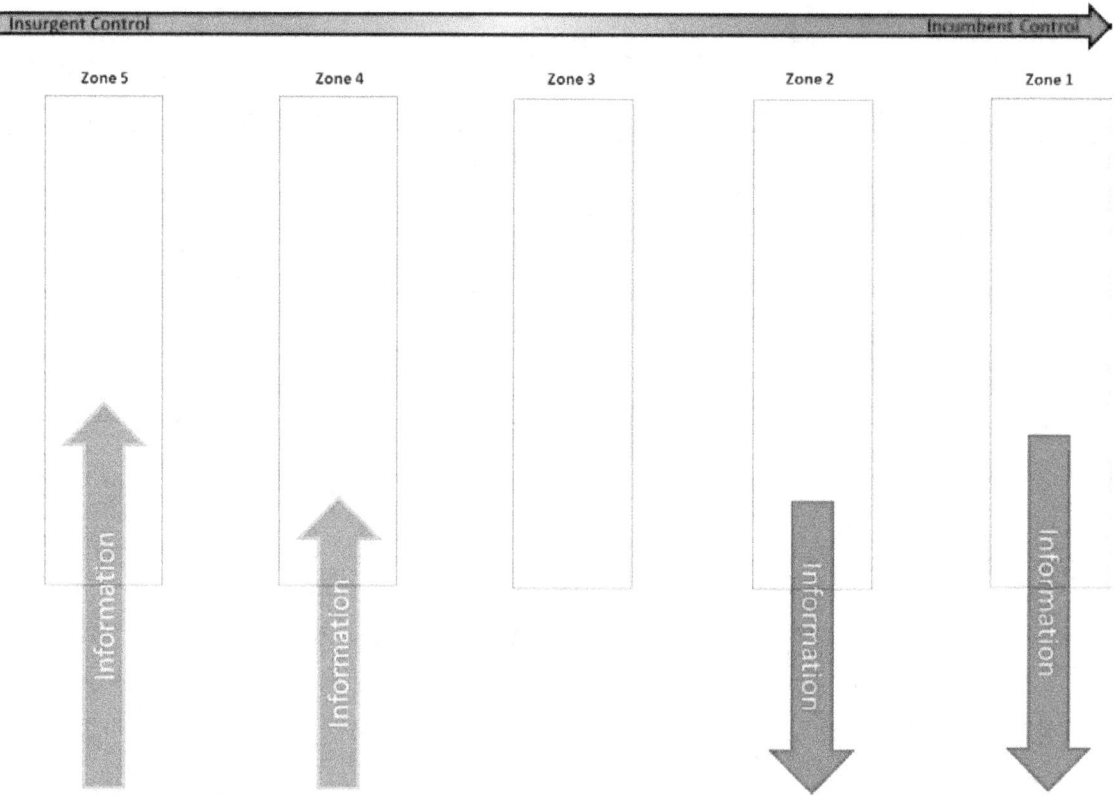

Figure 5.   Control and Information

Source: Created by author.

The levels of control and information displayed on the theory mirror Kalyvas's

definition outlined in chapter two of this study. Control is defined as an actor's ability to

reduce the likelihood that events will occur in certain areas at certain times (Kalyvas

2006, 210). The level of control possessed by the insurgent directly results in the level of

information the insurgent possesses in a particular zone. In areas of high control, the actor

possesses a high degree of information. In areas of low control, the actor possesses a low

degree of information (Kalyvas 2006, 210). The level of control and information within a

zone directly influences the remaining six components of the theory.

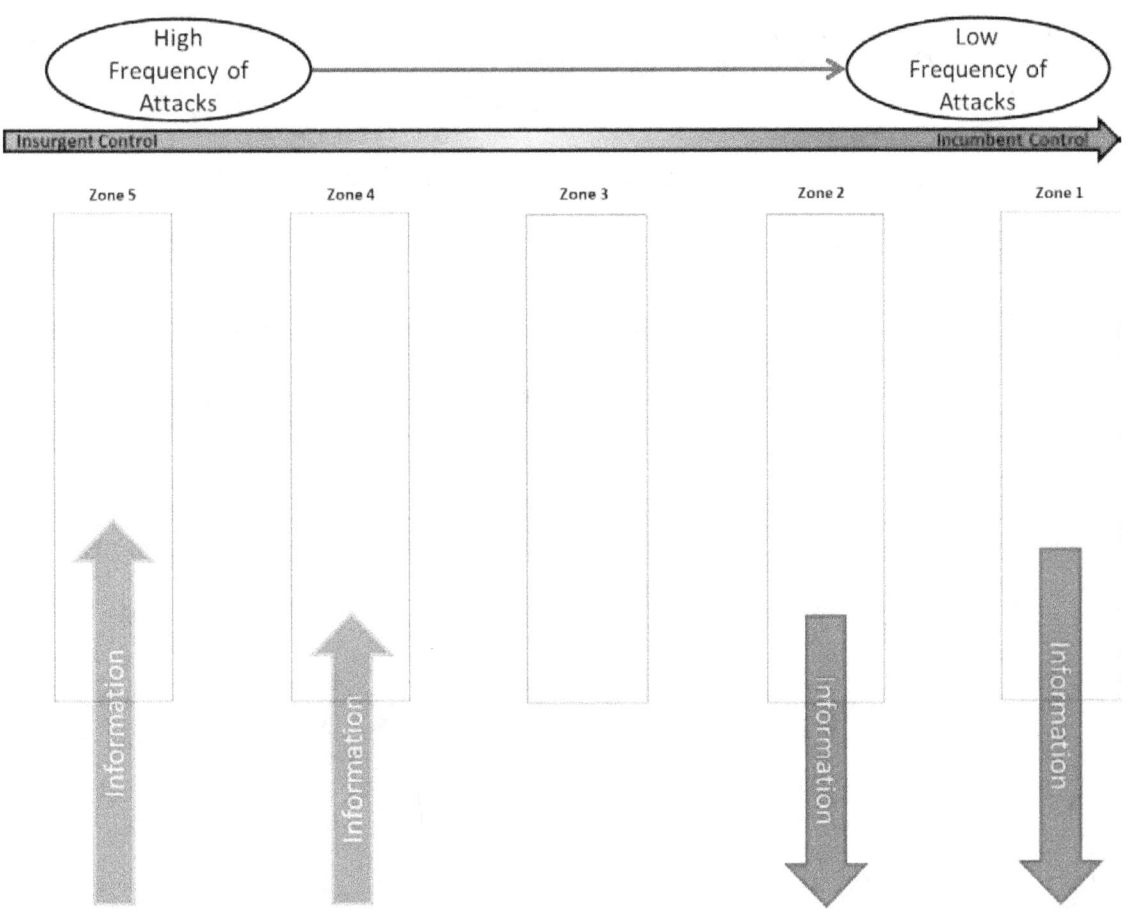

Figure 6.   Frequency of Attacks

Source: Created by author.

Frequency of attacks is displayed on the top of the theory with the most frequent

insurgent attacks occurring in Zone 5. The frequency of attacks reduces in each

subsequent zone until reaching the lowest attack frequency in Zone 1. This prediction is

based on supporting data generated from studies on attacks in Spain, Israel, Iraq, and the

Horn of Africa. LaFree's case study on the ETA demonstrated that attacks were

concentrated and contiguous when conducted from the Basque homeland (LaFree et al.

2011, 25). The ETA's attacks reduced in frequency as they shifted to a strategy of attacking further and further away from their base of operations (LaFree et al. 2011, 26).

The ETA's shift in attack frequency mirrors that of terrorist attacks in Israel. In a 2006

case study on the risk of terrorism across space and time, Claude Berrebi demonstrated

that attack frequency was substantially higher when conducted in close proximity to the

terrorist's base of operations (Berrebi and Lakdawalla 2006, 18). Townsley's studies on

insurgent attacks in Iraq and pirate attacks in the Horn of Africa offer additional support

to the prediction of frequency by demonstrating that attacks cluster in space and time in

zones that require the least effort of the insurgent and zones that support the optimum

forager.

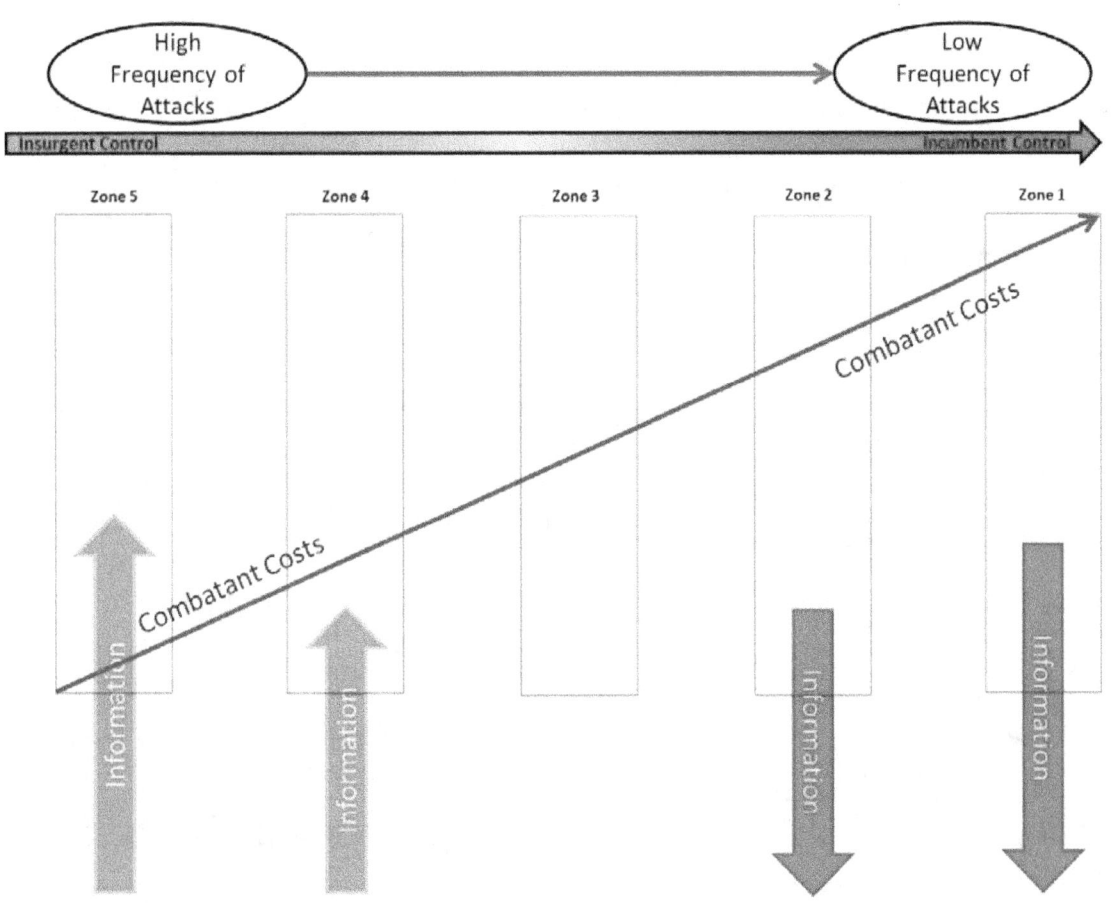

Figure 7.   Combatant Costs

Source: Created by author.

Combatant costs are defined as risk, time, effort, energy, training, manpower, distance, support, and information. These costs are displayed in the theory in the form of a diagonal line originating at the bottom of Zone 5 and concluding at the top of Zone 1. This line depicts costs at their lowest in Zone 5 and steadily increasing until they reach their highest point in Zone 1. Clarke uses September 11, 2001 (9/11) as an example of why proximity directly impacts costs (Clarke and Newman 2006, 142). In order for Al Qaeda to conduct 9/11 they had to infiltrate the United States with sleeper cells. These sleeper cells required the recruitment of individuals willing to sacrifice themselves, their covert insertion into the United States, finances to support their operations, combat and aviation training, and a long amount of time to complete the operation. Clarke points to these very costs as the reason that Al Qaeda is more likely to conduct attacks against U.S. targets overseas, rather than attempt a second attack the magnitude of 9/11 (Clarke and Newman 2006, 142). Berrebi's study on terrorist attacks in Israel compliments Clarke's thoughts and demonstrated that attacks cost significantly less in terms of "supply side" risk when they were conducted within close proximity of a terrorist base (Berrebi and Lakdawalla 2006, 18).

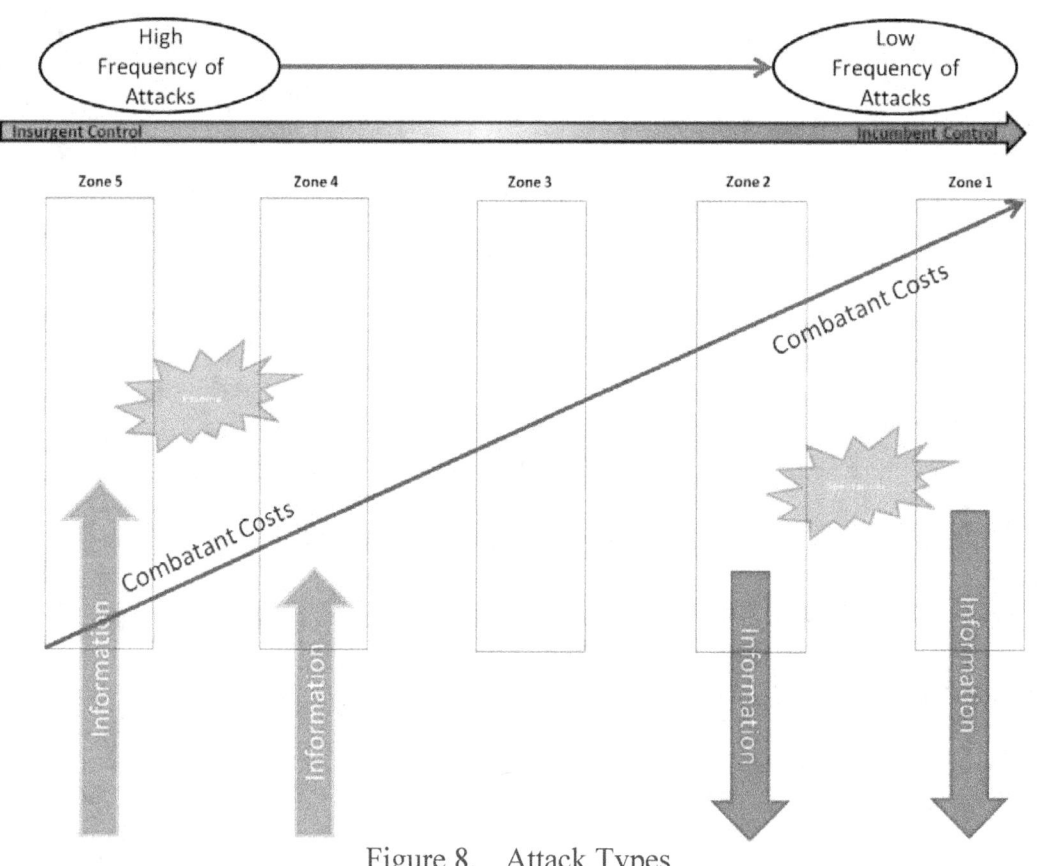

Figure 8. Attack Types

Source: Created by author.

The types of attacks depicted on the theory are routine and spectacular. Routine attacks are defined as events that are an established part of life that have limited impact on the population (Clarke and Newman 2006, 183). Spectacular attacks are defined as singular events designed to be high impact and maximize casualties (Clarke and Newman 2006, 181). Routine attacks are shown in areas of high insurgent control, while spectacular attacks are shown in areas of low insurgent control. This prediction is based on the insurgent's decision making process relating to the proximity of a target. Routine attacks flourish when the insurgents are conducting attacks near their base of operations (Clarke and Newman 2006, 157). They rely on a supportive population, information, and possess the time and facilities to conduct attacks on their own schedule. Attacks that occur far away from the insurgent's base of operations require considerable costs and must be larger in scope to compensate for their lower frequency (Clarke and Newman 2006, 141). An example of routine attacks can be found in the U.S. occupation of Iraq. Soldiers were transported from the protection of the United States to an environment in Iraq where they were much more likely to be attacked (Clarke and Newman 2006, 157). The attacks against U.S. soldiers became a routine event in the lives of the Iraqi citizens, were conducted near the insurgent's base of operations, and had a limited impact on the Iraqi population. An example of spectacular attacks can be found in the IRA's strategy following their inability to conduct routine attacks in England (Clarke and Newman 2006, 141). The IRA transitioned their attacks out of Ireland and into England, utilized larger bombs, targeted high profile members of the English Government, and attempted to disrupt the lives of the English population (Clarke and Newman 2006, 141).

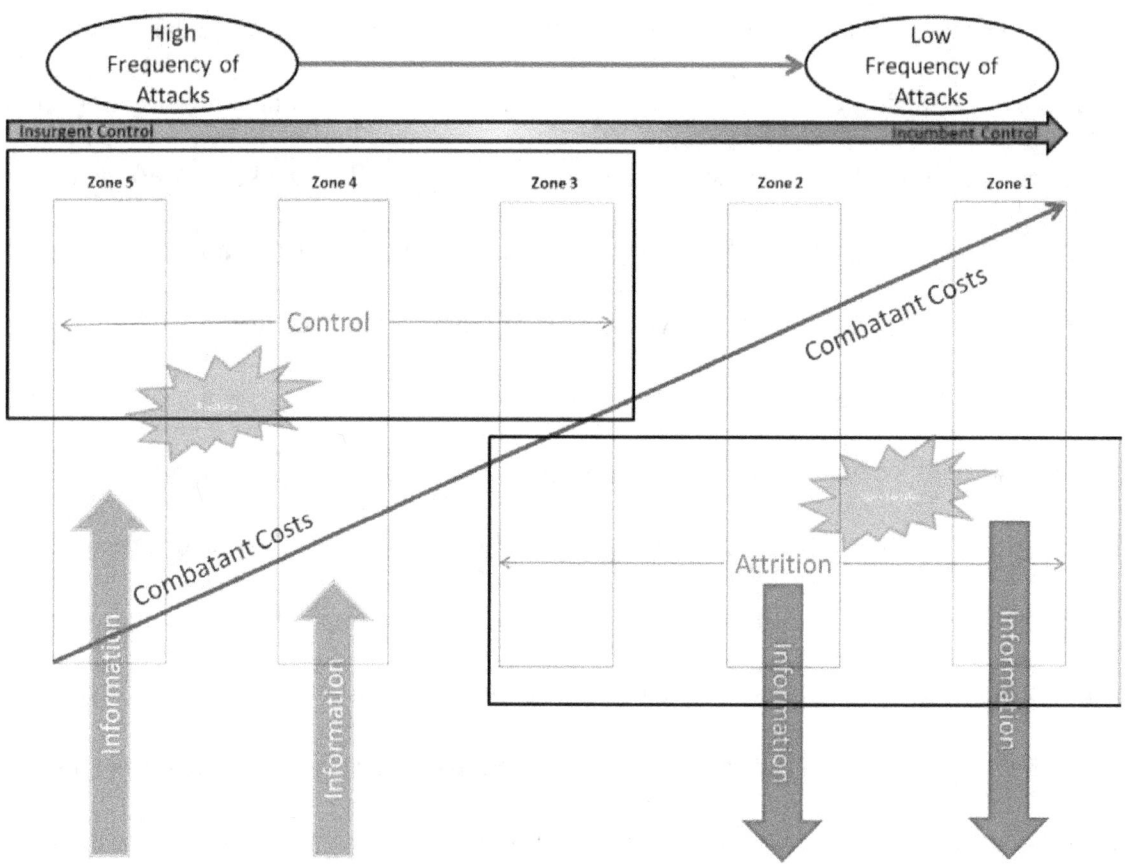

Figure 9. Organizational Strategy

Source: Created by author.

Organizational strategy is depicted on the theory as control and attrition. Control

and attrition are placed on the theory to reflect the findings of Gary LaFree's study on the

ETA from 2011. LaFree defined control attacks as those attacks that are designed to

consolidate and protect an organizations base of power (LaFree et al. 2011, 25). Attrition

attacks are those attacks that are aimed at wearing down an incumbent by striking at

locations outside of the insurgent's base (LaFree et al. 2011, 26). The strategy of control

resulted in concentrated attacks in contiguous areas while attrition resulted in dispersed

attacks across distance and time. Control attacks are positioned where the insurgents possess high degrees of control and attrition attacks are positioned on the theory where the insurgent has lower degrees of control. Zone 3 is depicted as having both attrition and control attacks due to the zone's state of flux between the incumbent and the insurgent.

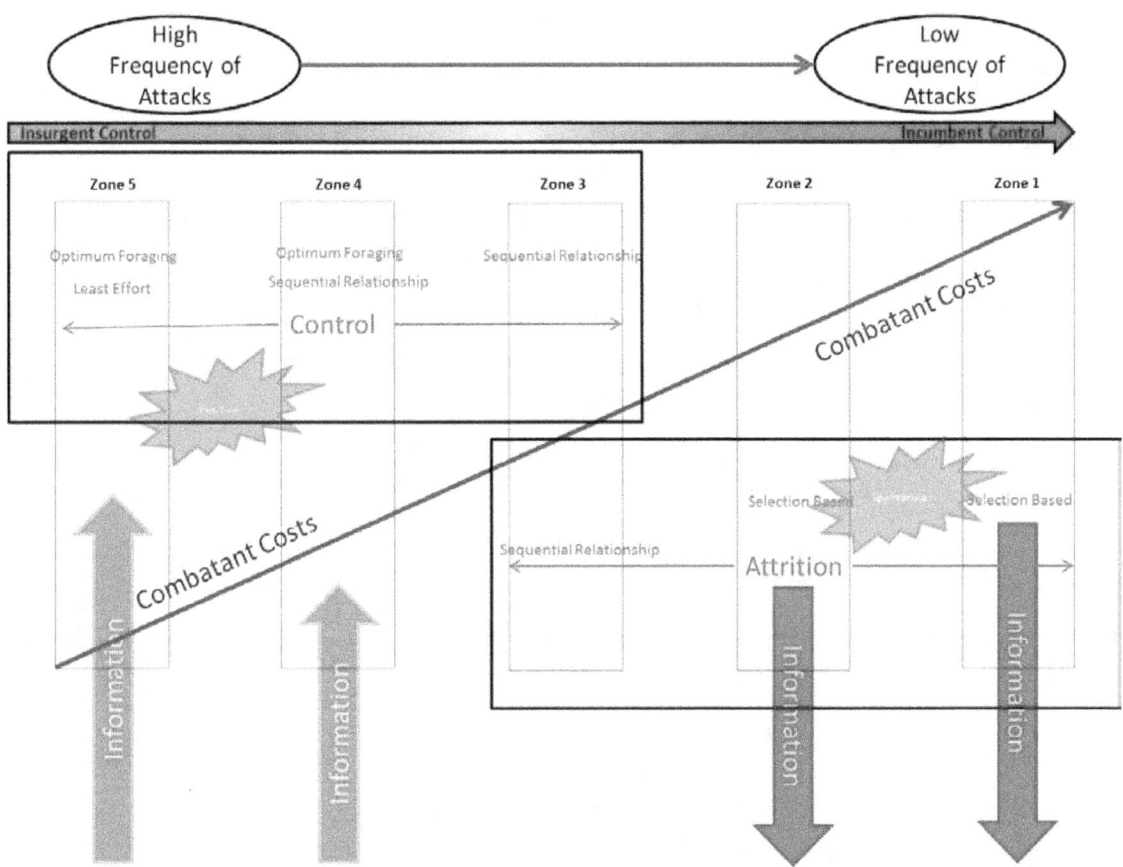

Figure 10. Causal Mechanisms

Source: Created by author.

The causal mechanisms of optimum foraging, least effort, sequential relationship, and selection are overlaid on the zones of control. These causal mechanisms, defined in chapter 2, are positioned based on the evidence demonstrated in their individual case studies. The optimum foraging principle and least effort principle occur in locations where the insurgent can conduct operations with minimum effort and maximum information. These locations are defined as Zone 5 and 4 on the theory. The sequential relationship principle states that the insurgent will attack where the incumbent is most likely to conduct operations. This location is identified as Zone 3 or the zone most often associated with the front lines of a conflict. Selection based targeting requires the insurgent to identify a target that will justify the combatant costs to conduct an attack. These locations are often found in the incumbent's area of operation and are placed in Zones 1 and 2 on the construct.

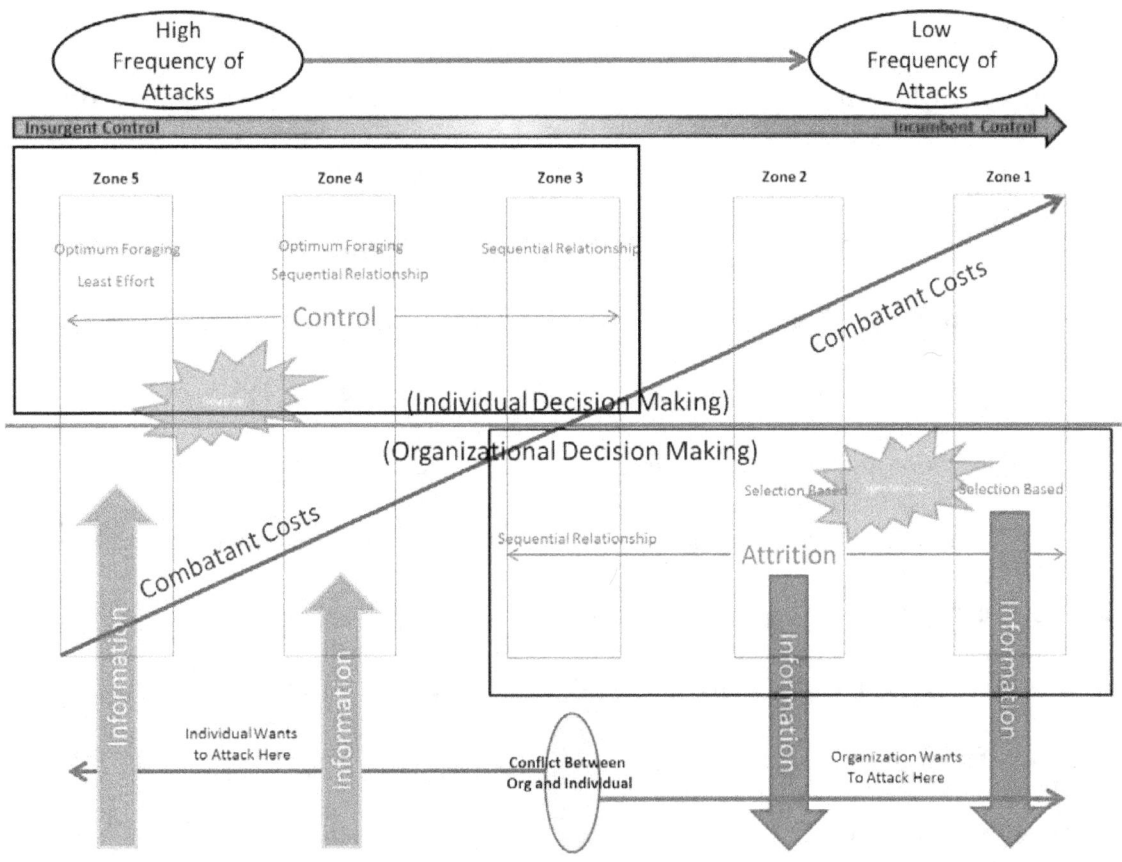

Figure 11. Individual and Organizational Conflict

Source: Created by author.

The final major component of the theory is depicted on the bottom of the slide

and predicts the potential conflict that could arise between the decision making process of

the insurgent and the insurgent group. This conflict is generated when the organization

desires to conduct attrition based spectacular attacks and the individual is not willing to

accept the combatant costs. The individual actor wants to conduct their attacks near their

base of operations where cost is relatively low. The organization wants to conduct attacks

in the incumbent's base of operations where the impact is relatively high. Zone 3 is

identified as the area that the individual may begin to resist the demands of the

43

organization and conflict occurs. This conflict played out in a 2011 news story by Carlotta Gall, where she detailed individual Taliban fighters' reluctance to follow orders to move into locations to conduct combat operations against ISAF (Gall 2011). The Taliban foot soldiers became angry at their Taliban leaders and began to question why men who were safe in Pakistan were willing to send so many to their death in Afghanistan (Gall 2011). The conflict that arose resulted in the splintering of several Taliban subgroups and the flat out refusal of junior leaders to fight (Gall 2011).

The eight major components identified in the theory provide insight into the decision making of insurgent groups and individual insurgents. This decision making process is driven by the causal mechanisms that vary across time and space depending on the level of control an insurgent possesses within a particular geographical area. The following subsections will discuss these geographical areas by utilizing Kalyvas's five zones. A distinct difference between this theory and Kalyvas results from the theory's focus on combatant against combatant violence compared to Kalyvas's focus on non-combatant violence. Kalyvas's predictions on systematic violence were focused on non-combatant violence and indicated that the more control an actor possessed, the less likely they were to conduct violence against non-combatants. I propose that the more control an insurgent possesses, the more likely they are to conduct violence against the incumbent representative. As control diminishes for the insurgent, causal mechanisms will alter, attacks will decrease, cost and severity will increase, and the potential for conflict between the organization and individual will also increase.

Zone 5

In 2006, the Taliban possessed total control of Zhari District, Afghanistan. Their fighters and leadership lived in the district and utilized it as their base of operations against Kandahar (Day 2008). The Taliban operated a shadow government and provided essential services, policing, and conflict resolution to the population. In turn, the population provided the Taliban with passive and active support in the form of finances, shelter, and manpower. The Taliban's dominance was so complete that they were able to adopt a conventional defense of the district and openly challenged ISAF authority in Regional Command South (Day 2008).

In September of 2006, the Canadians conducted operation Medusa in order to gain control of Zhari and limit the Taliban's ability to threaten Regional Command South (Day 2008). The Canadians would stage on Highway 2 and then drive south in an effort to clear the district of Taliban fighters (Day 2008). The Taliban were not surprised by the operation and their information dominance gave them knowledge of when and where Canadian troops were moving (Day 2008). The Taliban immediately responded to the Canadians' attempt to encroach within the district with harassing fire all along the border between the highway and district. Taliban fighters would aim their AK47s over the walls of their homes and simply fire at the Canadian troops on the highway (Day 2008).

Taliban fighters flowed from their bases within Zhari and engaged the Canadians throughout the Operation Medusa before acquiescing a narrow corridor that would eventually become the north south running Route Summit (Day 2008). Over the course of the next several months the Taliban would conduct routine attacks against Route Summit and inflict additional casualties on the Canadian forces. In the end, the Canadians and

ISAF were unable to commit enough combat forces to clear Zhari and the Taliban would retain the district as a base of operations for years to come (Day 2008).

Zhari District in 2006 demonstrated every component of Zone 5 from this chapter's theory. The Taliban had total control of the district and possessed a high degree of information. They knew when and where the Canadians were operating and they were capable of responding to any attempted encroachment within the district. The Taliban responded to the Canadian's penetration with harassment, guerilla, and conventional attacks that were routine and designed to retain as much control of Zhari as possible. Taliban fighters, supplied with an enemy within their own territory were driven by the least effort and optimum foraging principle and conducted attacks that minimized their costs while still offering a potential reward in terms of ISAF casualties. The individual Taliban fighter and the Taliban's overall decision making process remained in harmony because the least effort and optimum foraging principle complimented a strategy of control.

Although the Canadians were able to eventually secure small portions of Zhari, the Taliban retained control of the district for years to come. Their strategy of control remained in place and they continued to attack ISAF forces in a high frequency for years to come. This strategy would come to an end in 2010 when ISAF would dedicate enough combat power to change the balance of control in the district.

Zone 4

The transition from Zone 5 to Zone 4 sees the insurgent's total control reduced to a high degree of control. They can no longer enforce their dominance and prevent the incumbent from encroaching within the zone. This reduction in control results in the diminishment of the insurgent's information dominance and limits their ability to know when and where the incumbent is operating. The insurgent's levels of risk, time required, effort, training, manpower, distance travelled, and support to conduct attacks, all become costlier. The increase in combatant costs lowers the frequency of attacks and begins to alter the individual insurgent's decision-making process. The least effort principle no longer applies as uncertainty takes hold and attacks require a considerable amount of more effort to conduct. The optimum foraging principle remains, but its role as causal mechanism is reduced as risk is increased. The insurgent must travel further from his warren to conduct attacks and the rewards must be greater than they were within zone 5.

Zone 4 remains an insurgent stronghold, but as insurgent costs rise the causal mechanisms of the individual insurgent begin to transition. The least effort principle is replaced by the sequential relationship of insurgent and incumbent. The incumbents growing number of penetrations into the zone and the imperfect knowledge of when the penetrations will occur, results in opportunity playing a much larger role in target selection. The insurgent begins to rely on the incumbents movements and their sequential relationship becomes much more important.

Zone 4 also generates the beginning of conflict between the insurgent organization and the insurgent. The organization, still desiring to control their zone, pushes for more and more attacks despite the rise in attacks. This desire to increase attacks conflicts with the singular insurgents desire to reduce risk. The conflict that emerges in Zone 4 becomes readily apparent in Zone 3.

Zone 3

In June of 2006, the village of Alizai in Helmand Province, Afghanistan was the British army's frontline against the Taliban (Simpson 2013, 42). The British and the Taliban lacked control of the small village and competed for its support. The British conducted operations to clear out suspected insurgents, but local Afghanistan police commanders refused to accompany them for fear of reprisals (Simpson 2013, 43). The Taliban, operating out of Sangin, were unable to prevent the British from entering the village and turned to an increasingly violent campaign of assassinations against individuals associated with the Government of the Islamic Republic of Afghanistan (Simpson 2013, 45). The village's population, for their part, remained fairly neutral and had shifted their allegiance several times over the previous years. This alliance shifting was often dependent on local power players and their ability to finance the decision makers within the village (Simpson 2013, 44).

Alizai presents an accurate portrayal of Zone 3 from this chapter's theory. The Taliban and Government of the Islamic Republic of Afghanistan possessed equal levels of control of the village. Each rival travelled to the village to conduct their operations and neither was capable of establishing a foothold within the population. The local population attempted to side with whoever they thought had the greatest chance of success. When the population was unsure of who would dominate control, they transitioned to a weary passivity and attempted to remain neutral.

The Taliban's lack of control and information dominance in the region resulted in an increase in combatant costs. The Sagin based Taliban were forced to travel out of their zones of control and rely on the sequential relationship they possessed with Government of the Islamic Republic of Afghanistan to conduct attacks. These attacks decreased in frequency due to a lower level of opportunity, but transitioned to more violent attacks in the form of assassinations.

Alizai also shows the potential signs of conflict between the individual Taliban and the overall Taliban strategy. Taliban fighters traveling out of Sangin were forced to leave their home base and eventually began to lose control of Sangin to foreign based fighters. This resulted in an unsuccessful uprising against the Sangin Taliban in 2007 (Simpson 2013, 46).

Zone 2

Zone 2 alters the neutral state of Zone 3 and shifts the balance of control to the incumbent. The incumbent possesses a high degree of control and information and can limit the insurgent's encroachment within the zone. The insurgent's loss of freedom of maneuver and lack of knowledge of the zone results in their combatant costs elevating significantly. The increase in costs lowers the insurgent's ability to conduct attacks and shifts their overall strategy from one of control to attrition. Attacks alter from the routine to the spectacular to make up for the loss of frequency and enhance the attrition strategy.

The insurgent can no longer rely on sequential patterns of Zone 3 and 4 because they are required to conduct clandestine operations to avoid capture. Attacks transition to selection based targets that require increases in resources, training, manpower, financing, and time. The individual combatant now faces an extreme level of risk and their decision making becomes even more conflicted with the organization's attrition strategy. This is the first stage where the singular insurgent refuses to conduct operations for fear of death or capture. They can no longer rely on the safety of their base and the risks no longer offer the same rewards that were found in previous zones.

Zone 1

The introduction of this paper discusses Zhari District, Afghanistan in 2010 following the surge of ISAF into the region. The allocation of combat resources resulted in the Taliban fleeing the region, the population altering their passive and active support, and ISAF assuming dominant control of the district. ISAF's dominant control and high degree of information drove the cost of conducting operations to levels that most individual Taliban fighters were unwilling to accept. The Taliban's overall strategy in the area transitioned from control based routine attacks that used IEDs or harassing small arms fire, to fewer and deadlier suicide bomb attacks.

Zhari's dramatic transition from Zone 5 to Zone 1, in a period of a few years, highlighted the conflict that can arise between organizational decision making and individual decision making. The local fighters that fled Zhari had reached their limit in terms of risk and fled the region. Those fighters outside of the region, who had typically come to Zhari to conduct attacks, were no longer willing to return. The New York Times writer Carlotta Gall wrote in 2011, "Recent defeats and general weariness after nine years of war are creating fissures between the Taliban's top leadership based in Pakistan and midlevel field commanders, who have borne the brunt of the fighting and are reluctant to return to some battle zones, Taliban members said in interviews." Gall continued by saying, "During the fighting in the fall, the Taliban commanders sometimes found their calls for help going unanswered, according to American military officials. One group, in

Sia Choy, in the Zhari District of Kandahar Province, appealed for help from commanders to no avail" (Gall 2011).

Gall's articles on Zhari highlight the prediction that the insurgent and insurgent group enters a stage of conflict when combatant costs become too severe. These costs, borne of the insurgent's inability to control a zone and their lack of information concerning the incumbent's movement, continue to rise with the pressure of the organization's strategy to conduct spectacular attacks. In some cases, as in Zhari, the conflict can reach a point where the individual fighters flatly refuse to continue to fight.

Conclusion

What underlies the spatial and temporal patterns of insurgent attacks? This chapter combined the theories of criminology with Stathis N. Kalyvas's zones of control to form a theory that predicts the causal reasons of attacks. The eight major components identified on the theory impact the individual and group decision making process and show how they may come into conflict.

The analysis of the major components of the theory and their influence within the five zones provides insight on why attacks occur in spatial and temporal patterns. The next chapter of this paper will focus on this answer and provide a recommendation for future testing of the theory.

CHAPTER 5

CONCLUSIONS AND RECOMMENDATIONS

Conclusions

The theory presented in chapter four proposed that the causal mechanisms responsible for spatial and temporal patterns of attacks alter based on the level of control an insurgent possesses within a geographical region. The literature from Israel, Iraq, Spain, and the Horn of Africa leave no doubt that attacks cluster in space and time. This literature also supports the theory that those same attacks will diffuse as operations are conducted further away from an insurgent's base of operations. I propose that this diffusion is the result of increased combatant costs in terms of risk, time, effort, energy, training, manpower, distance, and support.

This theory, although untested in this paper, offers intelligence professionals insight into the decision making process of insurgents and attack patterns. We know that insurgents, pirates, criminals, and terrorists display common behaviors regardless of their cultural or ideological identities. This theory also offers insight on when and where the decision making process of singular insurgents may come into conflict with that of the insurgent group. We know that insurgents prefer to conduct attacks within the safety of their own operational area, but we also know that insurgent groups look to maximize terror by conducting spectacular attacks in an incumbent's base of operations. These conflicting desires offer a potential opportunity for military intelligence professionals to exploit.

The practicality of chapter four's theory can be observed in support of the four steps of the United States Army's intelligence process. Intelligence officers are responsible for conducting the four steps of the intelligence process; plan and direct, collect, produce, and disseminate (Department of the Army 2012). These steps overlap and support the operations process and can be enhanced through the theory presented throughout this paper.

The research and analysis step of the intelligence process consists of data collection and analysis in order to provide a commander with an accurate threat picture of the operational environment. Traditional intelligence preparation of the battlefield results in threat overlays, situation templates, event templates, and a host of pattern analysis tools. The failure of these products and those that brief them is that they are often presented as data sets without predictive or causal analysis. This paper's theory offers an opportunity to explain why events are occurring and an opportunity to rethink the presentation of data.

Threat overlays can be broken down into zones using historical attack data. Zones can predict attack types, attack frequency, causal mechanisms of behavior, and the strategy of insurgent organizations. Event templates can be developed based off of statistical data that shows future attacks will cluster in space and time. Pattern analysis wheels can transition from products that show when attacks have happened in the past, to tools that show caches will be located within close proximity of Zone 5 and Zone 4 attack locations, that bed down locations will be located within close proximity of Zone 5 and Zone 4 attack locations, and that attacks are statistically more likely to occur within certain periods of time.

The collection step of the intelligence process requires the tasking of intelligence, surveillance, and reconnaissance and combat power to answer the commander' priority intelligence requirements. The collection process is often the most difficult and criticized step within the intelligence community. This becomes most apparent following an attack and the resulting pressure from a commander to know when and where to allocate their assets. This paper offers a theory that can narrow search corridors and help define attack patterns. The intelligence officer who can tell their commander that a follow on attack will occur within one kilometer and within two days can significantly reduce search areas for combat patrols and collection priorities for intelligence, surveillance, and reconnaissance assets. An intelligence officer that can tell their commander that spectacular attacks in Zone 1 or Zone 2 are not likely to be followed by immediate attacks in nearby locations can equally save their commander's time in making decisions on how to posture their forces for follow on attacks. The theory presented in this paper helps intelligence officers formulate the "why" behind the data and articulate analysis capable of allowing their commander to make decisions.

The production step of the intelligence process takes the initial research from step one and updates it using the collection from step two. These products must be timely, accurate, predictive, and capable of supporting the commander's decision making process (Department of the Army 2012). These products must also help the commander understand why attacks are occurring. There has been a trend over the past several years to focus on cultural and ideological aspects of intelligence collection. These factors undoubtedly play a role in the motivation of why attacks occur, but this study shows that their role in the spatial and temporal patterns of attacks is greatly exaggerated. Attacks, more often than not, occur when the attacker is least vulnerable to risk and when opportunity presents a target. This explains why pirates in the Horn of Africa, criminals in the Netherlands, insurgents in Iraq, and terrorists in Spain all conduct their offenses in the same manner. Products that display these causal mechanisms offer commanders and soldiers insight to an insurgent's behavior and provide them greater clarity in understanding why attacks occur.

The dissemination step of the intelligence process provides the soldiers on the ground with products that help them understand the operational environment. These products are designed to provide the end user with the ability to make informed decisions on how to respond to their enemy's behavior. An infantry platoon that understands their patterned behavior results in the likelihood of increased attacks will alter their behavior. An infantry platoon that knows attacks occur within two days and one kilometer from a previous attack will operate more cautiously. An infantry platoon that receives products that explains, in basic understandable human terms, why an enemy behaves in a certain way, will be more likely to devise counters to potential future attacks.

Lastly, this theory has shown us a potential zone of conflict between the insurgent and the insurgent group. This conflict was highlighted in Carlotta Gall's New York Times' articles that featured Taliban commanders refusing the call to fight in zones they considered too dangerous. This conflict zone is an exploitable opportunity for intelligence operatives on the ground and for strategic level talks at the national level that attempt to leverage the weaknesses of an adversary.

Recommendations

This study proposes a theory on the behavior of insurgents and insurgent groups in a geographical area. It utilizes a multi-disciplinary approach that combines theories from criminology and the social sciences. These theories form a compelling story that explains the causal mechanisms behind spatial and temporal patterns in insurgent attacks. The predictions made in the theory have real world implications and provide value to the creation and understanding of intelligence products.

Unfortunately, the scope of this study does not extend to testing the theory against actual attack data. I recommend that future studies explore the theory presented in chapter 4 and test the attack types, attack frequency, and attack strategies of insurgents in geographic zones of control. These studies could potentially validate or invalidate the proposed theory. A case study would have offered additional credibility to this paper's theory, but limitations associated with time and available unclassified attack data restricted the potential of such a study.

The modern era of war has transitioned from state against state actors to small scale non-state conflict and internal civil wars. Accordingly, the academic community has shifted their focus to the behavior of insurgents and the causality of violence within civil wars. This paper attempts to provide an addition to that literature by proposing a theory that fills the knowledge gap on why a broad range of culturally diverse insurgents display similar attack patterns. This focus area is worthy of further study in the future and will continue to remain relevant to the United States military as long as we are tasked with intervention.

REFERENCES

Berrebi, Claude, and Darius Lakdawalla. 2006. How does terrorism risk vary across space and time? Rand Corporation Study. http://ssrn.com/abstract=964345 (accessed March 10, 2014).

Berman, Elie, and David D. Laitin. 2006. Religion, terrorism and public goods: Testing the club model. http://researche.create.usc.edu/nonpublished_reports/168 (accessed March 10, 2014).

Braithwaite, Alex, and Shane D. Johnson. 2011. Space-time modeling of insurgency and counterinsurgency in Iraq. *J Quant Criminol*, no. 28 (November): 31-48.

Clarke, Ronald V., and Graeme R. Newman. 2006. *Outsmarting the terrorists*. Westport, CT: Praeger Secuirty International.

Day, Adam. 2008. Operation Medusa: The battle for Panjwai. *Legion Magazine*, January 26. http://legionmagazine.com/en/2008/01/operation-medus-part-3-the-fall-of-objective-rugby/ (accessed May 22, 2014).

Department of the Army. 2012. Army Doctrine Reference Publication 2-0, *Intelligence*. Washington, DC: Department of the Army.

Flynn, Michael T., Matt Pottinger, and Paul D. Batchelor. 2010. Fixing intel: A blueprint for making intelligence relevant in Afghanistan. *Voices from the Field*, Center for a New American Security (January): 1-27.

Gall, Carlotta. 2011. In the Taliban's heartland, U.S and Afghan forces dig in. *The New York Times*, February 21. http://www.nytimes.com/2011/02/22/world/asia/22taliban.html (accessed December 7, 2013).

Kalyvas, Stathis N. 2003. The ontology of "political violence": Action and identity in Civil Wars. *Perspectives on Politics* 1: 475-494.

———. 2006. *The logic of violence in Civil War*. Cambridge: Cambridge University Press.

Kalyvas, Stathis N., and Matthew A. Kocher. 2009. The dynamics of violence in Vietnam: An analysis of the hamlet evaluation system (HES). *The Journal of Peace Research* 46, no. 3 (May): 335-355.

LaFree, Gary, Laura Dugan, Min Xie, and Piyusha Singh. 2011. Spatial and temporal patterns of terrorist attacks by ETA 1970 to 2007. *J Quant Criminol*, no. 28 (February): 7-29.

Matthews, Matt M. 2011. "Disrupt and destroy." In *vanguard of valor: Small unit actions in Afghanistan*, ed. Donald P. Wright, 131-156. Fort Leavenworth, KS: Combat Studies Institute Press.

Medina, Richard M., Laura K. Siebeneck, and George F. Hepner. 2011. A geographic information systems (GIS) analysis of spatiotempoeral patterns of terrorist incidents in Iraq 2004-2009. *Studies in Conflict and Terrorism* 34: 862-882.

Silverman, Barry G., Michael Johns, Jason Cornwell, and Kevin O'Brien. 2006a. Human behavior models for agents in simulators and games: Part I enabling science with PMFserv. *Presence: Teleoperators and Virtual Environments* 15, no. 2 (April): 139-162.

————. 2006b. Human behavior models for agents in simulators and games: Part II gamebot engineering with PMFserv. *Presence: Teleoperators and Virtual Environments* 15, no. 2 (April): 163-185.

Simpson, Emile. 2013. *War from the ground up: Twenty-first-century combat as politics.* New York: Oxford University Press.

Townsley, Michael, and Alessandro Oliveira. 2012. Space-time dynamics of maritime piracy." *Security Journal*: 1-13.

Townsley, Michael, Shane D. Johnson, and Jerry H. Ratcliffe. 2008. Space time dynamics of insurgent activity in Iraq. *Security Journal*, no. 21: 139-146.

Williams, Blair S. 2010. Heuristics and biases in military decision making. *Military Review* (September-October): 40-52.

Wilson, Margaret A. 2000. Toward a model of terrorist behavior in hostage-taking incidents. *The Journal of Conflict Resolution* 44, no. 4 (August): 403-424.

Zipf, George K. 1949. *Human behavior and the principle of least effort.* Oxford: Addison-Wesley Press.

www.ingramcontent.com/pod-product-compliance
Lightning Source LLC
Chambersburg PA
CBHW080541290526
45790CB00006B/2508